Flowers Every Day

Inspired florals for home, gifts and gatherings

Florence Kennedy

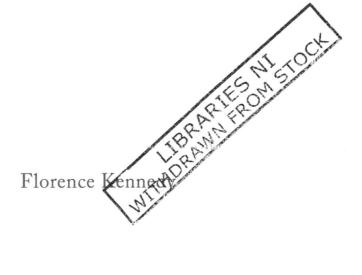
PAVILION

CONTENTS

—

INTRODUCTION

INTRODUCTION

I came to flowers quite late. It wasn't that I didn't like them; I just never really took the time to appreciate them or learn their names, let alone think about arranging them. Flowers felt like part of a world that I didn't belong to.

When I started Petalon, I was driven by the idea of delivering flowers by bicycle. The flowers were obviously a huge part of that but they were secondary to the basic business idea.

Then, overnight and quite unexpectedly, I became obsessed with the flowers and now I'm completely addicted – from finding new and achingly beautiful blooms I have never seen before, to creating colour combinations that sing and experimenting with textures and shapes, I'm hooked.

It's the nature of flowers that's so intriguing. Though there's a general understanding that a specific flower has a certain shape and colour, I think it's flowers' variations and imperfections that make them so beautiful. It's a treat to have a piece of nature inside your home: it should be celebrated for what it is.

Flowers are not naturally neat and tidy, so I don't really like to arrange them that way; it feels constricting and manicured, and goes against what I think flowers are all about. You can never be one hundred per cent certain that the flowers are going to behave in a particular way, and it's this uncertain quality that makes every arrangement unique.

I'm not classically trained in floristry. I've found this extremely useful at times and frustrating at others. It's useful because being self-taught means I'm not constrained by convention. I can do what feels right to me, and can break rules I never knew existed with ignorant bliss. I believe that it's much more important to arrange flowers in a way you think looks good and makes you happy, rather than in the 'right' way. On the downside, there are basic techniques which, had I known them, would have saved me a lot of time and effort, so I will cover some of these in this book.

I've loosely arranged the book into seasonal chapters, with five projects per chapter. The projects are not seasonally dependent so you can make a wreath in summer or a flower crown in winter; the flowers will be different but the methods will still be the same. These seasonal chapters show what incredible flowers are available at different times of the year and help you to see the choice that is out there.

Each project step-by-step is an informal guide that shows you the basics, but I urge you to experiment and explore different ingredients and textures: it would be boring if we all made the same thing!

On a personal note, I love acquiring a new skill and I hope to inspire others to do the same. I don't ever want to stop feeling that I'm learning more and more about flowers and how to work with them. I've found the joy of being creative with something that's natural is, by its very essence, ever-changing. I also think it's rather special to create something that will make others smile and improve their day.

So this book is for everyone who wants to embrace flowers. I hope it will encourage you to take the next step from buying supermarket roses to exploring your local flower markets and flower growers, through to foraging for those extra-special elements for your arrangements.

I also hope that this book will give you the confidence you need to use flowers to bring people together and to find your own way in a craft that is beautiful, challenging and, above all, natural.

ABOUT PETALON

Petalon is the name of my little flower delivery company in London. It is also responsible for my complete infatuation with flowers. The premise for the company is simple – we deliver beautiful flowers by bicycle all over London. There's a choice of two bouquets, which change each week depending on what's in season and what looks especially good at the flower market. And each bunch we sell includes a donation towards helping the bee population of our city.

At the beginning, I worked every aspect of the business, from going to the flower market, to taking orders, arranging bouquets and cycling around London delivering all the flowers. The business grew week by week, and we now have a fantastic team of florists, cyclists and studio managers, who work tirelessly to provide Londoners with fantastic flowers.

THE BASICS

SOURCING YOUR FLOWERS

There are endless options for sourcing your flowers and enjoying a wonderful mix of varieties, colours and smells throughout the year, but you need to be a little creative if you are to avoid bland arrangements. Although you can sometimes pick up great flowers at supermarkets, on the whole they sell the same flowers all year round. Flowers are also often flown in from far away, so think carefully before you purchase. So what are the alternatives?

Local florists

If you're lucky enough to have a good local florist, that's a great place to start. You can even ask your florist to order in certain flowers and foliage but be sure to do your research and select what's in season.

Local growers

You can also look online to find flower farmers in your corner of the world. There are more and more popping up and some will even deliver. A number will let you pick your own or they may have ready-picked bunches for sale. Here in the UK we have the British Flower Collective www.thebritishflowercollective.com, which is a great directory for finding locally grown flowers and lots of other interesting information around the industry.

Local flower markets

I use my local wholesale flower market for nearly all my flowers and foliage. It's an amazing experience going there but it's not for the faint-hearted.

You need to be there between 4am and 8am (the earlier the better) to get the best stuff, and you can't just buy one stem of this and one stem of that. The flowers come in wraps of five, ten, 20, 25 and 50, and you'll often be quoted the price per stem, so being able to do some quick maths is a must as it's easy to quickly go over budget. And remember, VAT is an additional charge. If buying large quantities makes things too expensive, consider going with a friend and splitting the cost.

Foraging & scrumping

Foraging flowers is a great way to get fantastic and unusual shapes and colours into your arrangements, providing you are foraging for your own use and not for commercial gain. Also, some land is covered by bye-laws, so watch for signage and check before you pick. In the UK, you are also prevented from picking certain plants, such as some orchid and fern species. But barring all that, when you're out foraging, be sure to have a bucket of water to hand for your new treasures and be mindful not to get carried away and snip into someone's property.

Another good source might be neighbours with an excess of garden flowers, but it goes without saying that you should ask permission.

THE BASICS

TOOLS & TECHNIQUES

Here are some basic tips and techniques, along with some essential tools to get you started.

Tools

There are all sorts of fancy tools for floristry, but these are the ones I can't live without for simple day-to-day use. A good, strong sharp pair of secateurs that allow you to handle everything from thick, woody stems to delicate vines and tendrils; chicken wire, which is really useful for larger arrangements to keep stems in place in a vase; lovely natural twine is a great way to secure your bouquets, although in some more fiddly work (mainly bridal) you may need to wire some stems; and I use baby sterilising tablets to keep the water fresh!

Conditioning flowers & foliage

When you get your flowers and foliage home you will need to condition them so that they last as long as possible and look their best. This involves stripping all the leaves that will sit below the water line in a vase or arrangement, or if you're making a bouquet, stripping the stems so they are clear of leaves from the bind point down. Remember, you can always take more leaves off but you can't put them back on again, so keep things on the leafy side, especially if you're worried about them looking a bit bare. It's also worth recutting the ends of the stems to allow a fresh flow of water up to the flower heads.

Next, you want to get the maximum usage out of each stem. With single-headed flowers that's relatively straightforward, but with foliage or stems with multiple flower heads, you need to think of the stem as a whole and work out how many usable pieces you can make from it. I call this sectional cutting and the length that you cut will depend on what kind of arrangement you're making.

A NOTE ON VASES

I don't really have strict rules when it comes to the scale and form of a vase as each flower looks different with a different vase. It's simply a case of working with what you have. Ask yourself: does that vase make the flower sing? Does it show off its best attributes?

If you have a tall, skinny bottle with a narrow neck, your arrangement is going to be rather vertical because there's a limit to how much you can angle the stems. To counteract any possible stiffness, use flowers with 'dancing' stems that have plenty of movement. A collection of bottles like this, filled with flowers such as fritillaries, dicentra and scabious, works wonderfully to create an effortless, light, airy arrangement with lots of height.

Short vases with open necks are trickier to work with, but for that effortless look, a large-headed flower like a rose or peony perched on the rim looks great. If I'm aiming for an arrangement that makes more of a statement, using a stocky vase with a big, open neck means I can maximise the angle of the stems and create a more horizontal, sprawling arrangement.

SPRING

SPRING

As each season rolls around, with it come all sorts of flowers and foliage that you haven't had a chance to use for a year. For me, the first glimpse of spring is when the trickle of late-winter blossoms on our streets seems to erupt overnight into endless, fluffy pink and white clouds. And then, when the first buckets of peonies make their appearance at the flower market, you know spring has officially sprung.

After the cold months of winter, with all their heavy-scented foliages, architectural bare branches, jewel-like berries and dried spices and seed pods, we slowly but surely move from working with sumptuous, velvety winter colour palettes to the light, airy, fresh tones of spring.

I still hold the same clichéd view of spring as I did when I was a child: chirping birds, bouncing lambs, greenery, sunshine and endless swathes of daffodils. But this joyous celebration of new life can also be expressed through flowers.

When spring arrives, I find myself greedily gathering up all the blossoming branches I can at the flower market – like spiraea, ornamental cherry and blackthorn – and naturally leaning more towards pale, sherbety shades, and lightness and brightness. With lots of whites, creams and pastel tones, everything has a real feeling of abundance.

It's also around springtime that homes start to fill with flowers again. Whether you've got a little snippet from the garden resting in a glass by the kitchen sink or a fistful of daffs on the dining table, there's real joy in that first rush of flowers and the hint of summer ahead.

In this section we will be looking at how to make flower crowns and big table arrangements, along with other seasonal projects that capture the essence of spring.

FLOWER CROWN

There's something wonderful about wearing flowers in your hair – probably because it only happens on very joyous and special occasions. The great thing about a flower crown is that it can convey different moods and feelings depending on the flowers you use and the density of materials in the crown. You could create a wedding crown using delicate, enchanting blossoms with plenty of tiny detail and intricate textures, as seen here; or a dramatic version, with deep, romantic colours and rich textures, full of ferns, seed pods and complex little flowers, that might suit an autumn or winter wedding; or a crown made from big, blousy, vibrant flowers, like the one on page 90, which would be perfect for a festival.

In other words, your crown can fit with whatever occasion you choose. The flowers I've used here are just a few examples of some of my favourite spring flowers, but each season offers endlessly changing possibilities.

The thing to remember with flower crowns is that the flowers aren't in water, and so sooner or later those beautiful blooms will flop. Some flowers do better out of water than others, so choose carefully and if you're worried, do a test beforehand.

The example here is a mixture of small-headed flowers and works well as a wedding crown. I've used some that will only last a few hours – I couldn't resist the spiraea and clematis straight from my garden – so it's best made on the morning of the wedding. I also used some tiny majolika spray roses, lovely little brown fritillaries with an ochre edge and the pips from an allium. For the foliage I've used eucalyptus tips; the leaves are much smaller at the tips and add to the textural effect I was after.

The crown will survive going down the aisle and will last through the bride having her pictures taken, but not much longer. However, the bride will be letting her hair down for the wedding party afterwards, by which time the crown no longer needs to look its best.

But if you're off to a festival or party, and want your crown to last as long as possible, then you need flowers that do well out of water. Some great choices to see your crown through the day are peonies, roses, carnations (don't turn your nose up – there are some amazing varieties these days), strawflowers, cornflowers, waxflowers, smokebush, globe thistles, lisianthus, viburnum berries, berried fruits, lavender, sanguisorba, allium pips (pips are the single flowers from a larger flower head), tuberose pips, hellebores, Santini chrysanthemums (these spray varieties come in some lovely, jewel colours) and hardy foliage, such as eucalyptus, myrtle, bay, rosemary and pittosporum. These are just a few examples, but I urge you to have a forage and experiment to see what you like, and how well it lasts before you make your final crown.

FLOWER SELECTION

Clematis
Spray roses
Fritillaries
Allium pips
Spiraea blossom
Eucalyptus tips

<u>1</u>

Wrap a length of strong, pliable wire once around your head to make the shape of the crown. Cut the wire a little longer than the circumference of your head.

<u>2</u>

Cover the wire with floral tape, pulling the tape taut as you go so that it becomes adhesive. Now you have the headband that forms the base of your crown.

<u>3</u>

Bend back the ends of the wire; these will become your fastenings for the crown.

<u>4</u>

Flowers that are very delicate or don't have a strong stem must be wired before you can attach them to the crown. There are lots of techniques: I usually either pierce the stem with a thin wire, then wrap the ends of the wire around the stem, or I make a 'hairpin' from thin wire, pierce the flower head with it, and then wrap the ends of the wire around the stem or use the ends to create a fake stem.

<u>5</u>

Tape all your flowers, wired or otherwise, onto the headband. Start at one end and add each flower so it overlaps the stem of the previous flower. You can cover the whole length of the headband with flowers or just the front if you prefer that look.

<u>6</u>

To secure your crown, either tie a length of ribbon to each end of the bent wire or simply wrap the ends of the wire together to form your circlet.

FLOWERS TO GIVE AS A GIFT

When I'm choosing flowers for a bouquet, they run through my mind as a sort of team. Each stem brings with it its own characteristics and together the flowers bring out the best in each other, whether that's in their tone, texture or form. A great way of creating interesting and beautiful bouquets is to include a mix of different flowers, herbs and foliages. By doing that you end up with plenty of texture, which I love.

For this hand-tied bouquet I've used a few of my spring favourites, all chosen for their different characteristics and unusual colours.

focal flowers
The showstoppers – the flowers that you base your
bouquet around.

supporting flowers
These will still be pretty outstanding, but will complement
the focal flowers rather than stealing their
limelight.

texture
Some little gestures to add intrigue and texture – berries, grasses,
a variety of flower forms and shapes. Not too much of the same,
though, as it can end up being a bit boring.

filler flowers
Some good background blooms.

foliage
I love to mix foliages rather than just sticking with one shade of
green; I might choose anything from vines hacked from the garden,
to ferns and rosehips, eucalyptus, hedgerow gems, and everything
in between. I love black and dark red foliages, too –
they are great for adding depth to your bouquet.

FLOWER SELECTION

Peonies

Eucalyptus

Mock orange

Nigella

Tulips

Ranunculus

Daffodils

Chives

Fritillaries

Sweet peas

Foxgloves

Larkspur

1

I like to start with a bit of foliage first, followed by a focal flower. As you include each stem, make sure it crosses over the previous one. I sometimes start a bouquet thinking one particular flower is the star but by the end, a different one has completely won me over, so don't overthink it too much.

2

Next I'll nestle in some of the other flowers, checking all the time that I'm happy with the mix of colours and the overall feel of my bouquet. Turn the bouquet round as you add each element and make sure the stems are all angled in the same direction so that your bouquet has a supportive, strong spiral of stems.

3

Keep turning the bouquet in the same direction and adding stems as you go. If you think the bouquet is likely to sit on a shelf or mantelpiece rather than on a table, there's no point wasting beautiful flowers that aren't going to be seen, so as you work, think about whether your arrangement will be viewed from the front or from all sides. Thread any thin stems through at the end so that they don't get damaged. Finally, tease out a few flowers to create a natural-looking arrangement, steering clear of ending up with a perfect dome of flowers.

4

Trim all your stems down to the same length, cutting each at an angle to maximise the cut surface area, which helps with the take-up of water. Keep the stems on the long side, especially as it's good to recut them throughout the week to keep your flowers looking their best.

5

Hold your arrangement firmly and tie your bouquet with twine, keeping the twine in place with your thumb and wrapping it around to secure your stems in place. Be careful not to tie the bouquet too tightly or you will break any delicate stems. To keep the petals protected while transporting the bouquet, wrap it in hessian, gift wrap or newspaper.

BUD VASES

The type of flowers and foliages that really enchant me are not petal-perfect. I like weathered roses that are streaked with character and smell like gardens. No two stems should behave the same way; I don't really get excited by a bunch of 20 identical, pristine roses.

I also think that the notion of nature's variety should extend to your vases. Different sizes, shapes and materials can be used together to create an easy, unmanicured look. I struggle to find vases that really captivate me, but trawling flea markets and charity shops has given me a treasured collection of bottles, jars and vases of all different shapes and sizes, with different patterns and varying degrees of wear and tear. Even using the same-shaped vase in different sizes gives your arrangement a more relaxed feel.

FLOWER SELECTION

Fritillaries
Dicentra
Ranunculus
Tulips
Apple blossom
Spiraea
Foxgloves
Roses
Double hellebores
Sweet peas

ARRANGEMENT

I like to get all my vases roughly in the positions they'll end up in and treat the collection as a whole arrangement rather than as lots of individual ones. That way everything connects much more easily and you can make sure the flowers and vases sit well together. The nice thing with bud vases is that they are relaxed and take minimal effort to fill.

Here I've used a mix of spring flowers of varying shapes and sizes to create a light and airy feel. Worth a special mention are the three different types of fritillaries with incredible swooping stems, dicentra with their strings of dainty, dangling, heart-like flowers and the soft, ruffled petals of ranunculus.

BIG VASE

Big vase arrangements are my favourites. I end up treating them more like sculpture, thinking about which branches or stems will dictate the shape, how it will all come together as naturally as possible and where the negative space will be. In all types of art, it is the negative space that highlights the shape and the various elements of the design, and that creates the most stunning work.

I also love that these arrangements never end up looking quite as you thought they would – but that's the nature of working with nature.

These bigger arrangements look great as statement stand-out pieces and can command a room when placed on a plinth or side table. They are a fantastic way to showcase the best of the season's flowers and give you a chance to use some of the bigger, more dramatically shaped flowers and foliage that don't necessarily fit into a hand-tied bouquet.

Bowl-shaped vases like the one I've used here are a lot of fun to work with. Their big, open necks mean that you have a lot of scope for exploring more horizontal shapes and more freedom to add interesting details. I love to have flowers, foliage, fruit or berries draped over the vase edge on one side, and big, looping vines and stems arching across the other. But every arrangement offers a chance to explore the different characteristics of your flowers and to find different forms you like. Part of the joy for me is the sense that when I make these arrangements, I never stop learning about the flowers and about the process.

I used geranium leaves to build the base of this arrangement; they smell incredible, the leaves are fantastically shaped and they possess a natural variety of size, form and colour, so nothing ends up looking too neat. The jasmine and the sweet pea vines give the arrangement its sprawling shape and the never-ending ruffles of petals from the roses and the peonies make the piece look incredibly ample and abundant.

Just a tip: I like to rest my foxgloves on the rim of a bucket before I use them to encourage them to bend and curve interestingly instead of standing on their usual, poker-straight stems. It can be hard using lots of straight, vertical flowers in a large arrangement without it ending up looking too much like a firework.

FLOWER SELECTION

Geranium leaves

Jasmine vines

Sweet pea vines

Roses

Peonies

Foxgloves

1

Ball up some chicken wire and tape it securely to your vase with pot tape. You want the chicken wire dense enough that it will hold the stems in place, but not so dense that you can't get the stems in properly.

2

Start to place the foliage and structural branches that will dictate the shape of your arrangement. Keep it loose and take a step back every now and then to make sure you're happy with the shape the arrangement is taking.

3

Start to add your focal flowers, making sure to place them in clusters and at different heights. You want them to look natural so try not to position them too evenly through the arrangement.

4

Add your supporting flowers and the little textural details. Be sure to insert them at different depths so that everything looks easy and natural. I leave the vines to the end so I can drape and string them through the arrangement.

TABLE MEADOW

Flowers can either add quietly to the atmosphere or they can take centre stage and create a show-stopping setting for an occasion, be that a surprise brunch for your recently engaged best friend, the arrival of a new family member or your grandparents' fiftieth wedding anniversary. Occasions such as these call for more than just a gesture. This table meadow ticks all the boxes.

When planning this arrangement, think about how your table is going to be used. It might be to host a buffet lunch, in which case the height of the arrangement isn't critical. But if it's for a sit-down meal, people will want to talk to each other across the table and then your meadow must be height-restricted otherwise it can be rather antisocial. And if people are to be seated around the table, you will need to make sure your arrangement looks equally fantastic from both the front and the back, whereas if the arrangement is only going to be seen from the front, then there's no point working on the back.

The great thing about this design is that it's incredibly versatile. Depending on your table and the room, this meadow piece can be tall and willowy, short and flowing, abundantly full, or sparing and architectural.

There are no right or wrong choices for this piece but I recommend using good foliage or blossom to get the coverage you need while keeping things light. If you cover the floral foam with nothing but flowers, it can not only get incredibly expensive but will also change the nature of your design and can make things look overcrowded. I've used mock orange and spiraea to get a loose, easy shape that manages to cover most of the floral foam.

Don't let the word 'meadow' in the title restrict you. You could have a big, blousy arrangement with lots of fluffy peonies and rambling garden roses sprawling across the table. These larger-headed flowers are great for filling lots of space and creating a refined, romantic feel.

If, on the other hand, you want to create a bucolic look, then the garden and the hedgerow are great places to start. From where I write this, I can look outdoors and see lots of ferns in a spectrum of colours, brambles with crinkly white blossoms (make sure to wear a good pair of gardening gloves), honeysuckle clinging onto bushes and dog rose dotted throughout the roadside. Just think about the shape of each stem and how it will work with your arrangement.

FLOWER SELECTION

Peonies

Fritillaries

Roses

Ranunculus

Poppies

Daffodils

Mock orange

Spiraea

Anemones

Aquilegia

Apple blossom

Tulips

Hellebores

1

You will need trays and floral foam to fit your space. Line the foam blocks up on the table to see how many you'll need; they don't have to sit flush with one another as the foliage and flowers will cover any gaps. Soak your floral foam in a deep sink by laying the blocks on the surface of the water and letting them sink. Don't push them down. When they're fully saturated, take them out and place them in the trays.

2

Create the basic shape for each tray using the foliage, filler foliage and blossom, plus a few key flowers so that you can see where your focal points will be. Each stem must be conditioned and the lower leaves removed (see pages 14 and 186). The arrangement will look sparse at the beginning but don't be tempted to overcrowd things: you can always go back and fill any gaps later on.

3

Start filling out the piece with your assortment of flowers and foliages. Place the flowers so that they are at varying heights and angles to give the arrangement a sense of movement. Be sure to work with the shape of the flowers and their stems so that everything feels as natural as possible.

4

When you're happy with the overall shape and composition, scan the arrangement for any visible floral foam and cover it with more flowers and foliage. Line up the finished trays on the table and do a final check for any gaps. Take extra care to make sure that the base of the arrangement, where it meets the table, is covered, too.

SUMMER

SUMMER

For me, summer is encapsulated in hazy fields of bleached grass, sun-drenched days, colourful, flower-filled gardens, open-air parties, lazy lunches of salads and fruits, and an endless flow of drinks and conversation.

I find myself using much warmer colour palettes for my summer work: lots of bright, fruity colours, corals and oranges, cherry reds and plums. I love reflecting the seasons in flowers, and with so many wonderfully coloured flowers at this time of year, it's easy to do so.

The bittersweet nature of working with seasonal flowers is saying goodbye for another year to some of my favourite spring flowers. But peonies are still around for the start of summer and I love to work with the really juicy varieties like 'Coral Charm', 'Coral Sunset' and 'Peter Brandt'.

Then there is the crossover of seasonal flowers and getting to use the first dahlias with the last peonies is such a treat. I feel that dahlias mark the beginning of summer and I'll use them continuously throughout summer and autumn.

In the past, dahlias have been considered a bit naff but there are now some incredible varieties, with beautiful muted tones and in all shapes, from ombré pompoms to single-petalled varieties with smiling centres. Nearly every bride has 'Café au Lait' dahlias on her wishlist these days; they are an incredible nude colour with streaks of soft pinks that lick the petals like flames. They can also grow to the size of your face so they pack quite a punch.

The London flower market is awash with English flowers in summer. There are buckets of multicoloured dahlias, iridescent stalks of verbena, happy little marigolds, scabious of all shapes and sizes, cosmos and sweet-smelling English Roses, whose scent, range of colours and daily changes in appearance make them among my favourite flowers. Unlike their Dutch counterparts, English Roses have an imperfect charm that is utterly captivating.

It's also around this time of year that I can start to use branches dripping in fruit – great for bigger pieces, but also fun as small offcuts in bud vases and bottles.

FLOWER CHANDELIER

This is what we call a blockbuster. If you're celebrating an important event and want something a bit different and extra-special, then this guy is the one. It's a great way to show off some of the best flowers of the season and really play with the structure and character of each of the flowers and foliage. This is when you've got to think in 3D more than ever, bearing in mind when you are designing it that your arrangement will largely be seen from below.

Big, open peonies really come into their own in a large arrangement like this. They are great for acting as the main focus as well as for filling space. Another bonus is their incredible array of changing colours. Other large summer flowers that would work well as alternatives are hydrangeas or dahlias.

As you add the flowers and foliage, vary the depth at which you place them so that the finished arrangement has movement, rather than just ending up as a lump or ball. I've used clouds of achillea and little dancing daisies for texture, and have punctuated the sea of peonies with rich English Roses.

If you are planning to make this or something similar, just be sure that your support – be it a rafter or hook – is strong enough, as this hanging installation can get pretty heavy.

FLOWER SELECTION

Peonies

English Roses

Sweet pea vines

Hornbeam foliage

Blackberries

Achillea

Prunus

Apple branches

Tanacetum daises, a mixture

Rosehips

1

Cover your floral foam ball in chicken wire and secure it with cable ties or wire.

2

Cut a piece of strong wire long enough to be doubled and then threaded through the floral foam ball.

3

Fold the wire in half like a hairpin and, treating the doubled wire as one piece of wire, push it into the floral foam ball.

4

Be sure not to pull it the whole way through, but instead leave the loop exposed at the top. Separate the two pin legs, fold each one back over the chicken wire and twist them tightly to each side of the loop. Soak the floral foam ball in water, then hang it up to work on it. To do this, attach a carabiner clip to the wire loop and through the chicken wire for extra strength. Tie your rope to the carabiner clip.

5

When your floral foam ball is hanging and well secured, start inserting the architectural foliage branches into the foam. These will dictate the shape of your arrangement.

6

I'm not too fussy about the order I work in after that. I use a little of everything to build up a sense of the character I want, being sure to give each element space to be seen. Just remember, this arrangement is on a big scale so it's a nice opportunity to play with bigger flowers and interesting shapes.

BUTTONHOLES

I love buttonholes. They are the sweetest little gestures, like miniature bouquets. They can also celebrate the tiny offcuts and 'forgotten' flowers that might otherwise be considered filler or scraps. You can even wire up small stemless elements (delphinium petals and allium pips (see page 26) are real gems) into buttonholes or gather up a collection of dried grasses, side shoots, rosebuds and seedheads.

There are a few things to remember when you make a buttonhole. It is going to be out of water all day, so the flowers you choose and how far in advance you make the buttonhole are really important. If I'm wiring buttonholes, I'll do it as late as possible but you can sit unwired buttonholes in a cup of shallow water if you want to make them in advance.

Typically, buttonholes are used for weddings, where there is a whole lot of hugging, so these little chaps are going to be put through their paces and will probably be squashed rather a lot. So choose tough flowers or support softer petals with a backing of strong foliage or with flowers that can act as mini shock absorbers.

You might like to play with adding slightly larger or more brightly coloured flowers to act as focal points to your buttonholes, or to introduce some little berries, waxflowers or dried grasses, to add texture and a touch of intrigue.

Buttonholes are a lovely way to accent colours in people's clothing or ties on big occasions, or to add a bit of colour if needed. You can finish the buttonhole with a tie of ribbon, string or twine to set the mood or add to the gesture.

Mostly you will secure a buttonhole to clothing using a pin but lightweight buttonholes can actually be 'posted' through a buttonhole on a dress or jacket.

When it comes to size, less is more. Keep your buttonholes small and light.

FLOWER SELECTION

Clematis

Spray roses

Fritillaries

Alliums

Spiraea

Eucalyptus

1

Collect your offcuts and any 'forgotten' flowers that are too short to go in any other arrangement. Recut the stems and give them a good drink of water.

2

Gather up your ingredients into a mini bouquet, making sure any flowers that might droop are propped up by stronger berries or foliage. If necessary, you can wire flowers for buttonholes to give them extra support (see the spring Flower crown on page 29).

3

Remember that a buttonhole is a front-facing arrangement; it's easier to see everything if you place any taller, broader leaves at the back as a sort of frame, with shorter elements at the front. But the beauty of buttonholes is that they look just as lovely as little clusters, so don't worry if you don't fancy any bigger bits of foliage.

4

I secured my buttonhole with a length of floral tape, but string works well, too. You could also use fancy ribbon if the occasion calls for it. Finish by trimming all the stems to the same length, and you're good to go!

CHAIR DECORATION

Chair decorations are a great way to celebrate special guests at a gathering. They are most frequently used for the happy couple at a wedding, or for birthday or anniversary celebrations.

Here we look at making a chair decoration with fresh flowers that will last all day, but you can also make simple decorations with hardy flowers and foliage like rosemary and waxflowers, which don't need floral foam soaked in water, but can be wired straight onto the chair.

The arrangement pictured here is made up of a collection of some of my favourite summer ingredients. I love the juicy, fresh green of scented geranium leaves. Their unusual shape adds a unique texture and looks great against the bright summer colours of the dahlias and roses. They also smell incredible.

There are endless kinds of dahlias. I love to mix pompom varieties with delicate, single-petalled ones with smiling yellow centres. The natural ombré colouring of some of the dahlias I have used makes them great transition flowers that work to form a link between the different coloured elements of the arrangement.

Vines winding down chair legs or looping through the framework of the chair are a really fun way of accentuating the decoration, making it look as if it's actually growing on the chair. Seed pods and berries always add interest and texture and I love using them. It's so exciting to spot little apples or fruit in floral work; they feel like a celebration of nature as a whole – a world away from the notion of a generic floral arrangement.

Remember that it's important to choose the right chair. You need to be able to secure the floral foam, which means that an arrangement like this isn't going to work with a chair with a solid back.

FLOWER SELECTION

Geranium leaves
Hornbeam
Dahlias
Marigolds
Echinaceas
Roses
Jasmine
Sweet pea vines
Small apple branches
Seed pods
Berries
Rosehips

1

Here I've used a small offcut of floral foam wrapped in chicken wire, but you could use moss wrapped in chicken wire or even little floral foam cages that are specially designed for this kind of work. If you are cutting your foam to size, you can make the piece as big as you like and whichever shape works with the chair you've chosen. Soak the floral foam and attach it to the chair using wire or cable ties. Remember that the flowers will make the final arrangement quite a bit bigger than the foam, so position it with this in mind.

2

Start by placing your base foliage to create the overall shape. Make sure each stem is securely held in the floral foam and isn't sticking out through the other side, or it won't get a drink and will quickly droop.

3

Begin adding your flowers. I don't really have a preference about which size or texture of flower to place first. Just use a little bit of everything so that you build the arrangement up gradually, getting an idea of the character and shape of the piece as you go.

4

Make sure you can't see any foam. If there are any gaps, just fill them with flowers or foliage. You should also avoid using delicate flowers that will get squashed or berries that will stain someone's clothes when they sit on the chair. Instead use a hardy filler, such as some evergreen foliage.

FESTIVAL FLOWER CROWN

Here's another example of using flowers for a crown. It employs the same technique as the Flower crown on page 29, but this one is a real statement piece, with bigger wired flowers than the spring version. These flowers will last all day, which makes the crown perfect for parties and festivals.

With larger flowers like these, make sure you use strong wire and tape the ends of each stem to maximise their longevity. I like to nestle them gently together so the flowers provide support for each other. That way, even when they start to go soft, they don't really droop.

SUMMER TABLE FLOWERS

There's nothing quite like enjoying a big summer spread with your nearest and dearest outside in the sunshine. I love the laid-back character of the season and the chance to bring a slow, easy, just-gathered feel to its flowery offerings. Add in summer's amazingly coloured fruits and vegetables, and decorating a table has never been so easy. A collection of mismatched vases and bottles holding the flowers enhances the informality and ease of sharing platters, and of heaped plates overflowing with fresh salads, ripe fruit and other colourful offerings.

I love making table arrangements like this one – rambling, carefree and perfect for informal dining. Although I might use lots of individual containers, I think of the table as a whole and make sure nothing is too perfect and that no two identical arrangements are next to each other. I also try to avoid having a neat series of same-sized arrangements. They can end up looking too formal and take away from the character and rhythm of the setting.

What I do like is to contrast little bud vases nestled low against the table with vines sweeping high across the rest of the flowers. This keeps the skyline varied and undulating, helped by the addition of architectural highlights like single, slender stems of chocolate cosmos jutting out from the crowd, or twists and twirls of some scabious seedheads. Details like these celebrate the flowers' individual characters and punctuate the busy mass of bigger flowers and foliage in the display.

The lovely thing about these summer colours is that they all work so well together. I've used a lot of peach and apricot shades on this table. They melt effortlessly into coral and berry tones as well as fading into creamy yellows and soft blushes.

FLOWER SELECTION

Dahlias

Echinaceas

Sweet pea vines and flowers

Hornbeam

Blackberries

Achillea

Scabious

Geranium leaves

Chocolate cosmos

Dill

Apple branches

Marigolds

Tanacetum daisies, a mixture

Nigella

1

Place an assortment of vases, bottles and jars on the table, being sure to mix heights, sizes and shapes to create an easy, flowing feel. Take care to fill them with plenty of water; if the weather is hot, your flowers will need a lot to drink.

2

Instead of filling one vase at a time with flowers, work on the table as a whole, mixing textures, colours and shapes as you go.

3

As you get into it, you'll find you have a tendency to focus heavily on one area, so keep stepping back from the table to view it in its entirety.

4

It's lovely to end by linking the vases with long tendrils and swooping vines. I've used sweet peas here, but jasmine, clematis and passion flower vines are all great, too.

AUTUMN

AUTUMN

Autumn is that magical time of year when there's still warmth in the sun and a return of freshness in the air after the sticky heat of summer. It's the most dramatically picturesque season, with the sudden turning of the trees from the bright, chlorophyll-rich greens of spring and summer to an array of golds, silvers and bronze, and with rich, rusty red and crisp, curling brown leaves carpeting the floor.

There is something about the beauty of the imperfect that constantly pulls at my heartstrings and that makes working with nature such a joy. Autumn lends itself to this imperfect beauty with such ease, the leaves giving us all shades of fiery colours, the grasses and seed pods brittle and dried after summer, berries aplenty to work with – and all paired with the flowers that thrive at this time of year. It's a unique and exciting palette to work with.

Harvest is traditionally a big part of autumn, and you can reflect this beautifully when you're working with flowers. I think that as long as they look beautiful, fruits and vegetables should be used in flower arrangements, too. They can really stamp the season on an arrangement and help to showcase nature's best stuff.

I love using little strings of cherry tomatoes dripping over the edge of a low lipped vase, or a pomegranate or fig sliced in half and resting at the foot of an arrangement to emphasise the colours in the flowers. Mixed with dried hops and autumn flowers like dahlias or heirloom chrysanthemums, or with the last of the hydrangeas and roses, the arrangements at this time of year feel incredibly rich and abundant.

BRIDAL BOUQUET

Autumn colour palettes don't have to be all reds, rusts and browns, especially if you want something a bit 'bridal' for your wedding day. Here, using the same basic technique as on page 37, I've used a muted palette of off-white, creamy coffee and golden mustard, with nude tones and flashes of silver. I've included strawflowers left over from summer but dried to give texture and to add an impression of autumn. I've also kept the foliage very minimal and chalky to soften everything and add to the ethereal, understated feel of the bouquet.

Bridal bouquets are such a wonderful tradition and are one of my favourite things to make (but probably also the most stressful). The bouquet can completely alter the whole character of the wedding. If you go for blousy roses and minimal foliage, everything inevitably feels a little more formal. But if you use lots of foraged foliages and seed pods, and interesting little pieces, then a bouquet instantly feels more relaxed and a little wilder. There is no right or wrong; my wedding bouquets are designed around the bride's character, the venue and her choice of dress.

I'll usually design bridal bouquets with a front and a back. Although I tell my brides which way to hold their bouquet, there's a lot on their minds that day so it's safer to make the back just as lovely as the front, so that no matter which way the bouquet is held, it still looks beautiful.

With regards to shape, I tend to stay clear of domed or rounded bouquets, which look rather formal. Instead, I prefer more of a horizontal shape so that, when the bride is no longer walking down the aisle, she can hold her bouquet loosely at her side and it gives a more relaxed appearance.

FLOWER SELECTION

Dahlias
Hydrangeas
Strawflowers
Limonium
Roses
Mimosa
Lisianthus
Achillea

LIVING STAIRCASE

Staircases are my favourite – and among the simplest – things to decorate. They deliver such a wonderful impact. They are also a fantastic example of how your choice of flower can completely dictate the mood, no matter how big the scale of the arrangement.

This installation just goes to show you don't need a big, fancy double staircase to create a beautiful effect. The narrow, rickety staircase decorated with meadowy, muted tones is one of my favourite pieces in this book, and it was one of the simplest to make.

I used tall, vertical flowers that had plenty of texture and avoided large, prominent flower heads, like roses, to achieve a more meadow-like effect.

Daucus is a beautiful off-white shade, but I've also used the 'black' variety, which adds some depth and connects with the other, more autumnal tones in the piece. Then there are also some dancing sanguisorba and dried scabious seed pods, soft grey-blue globe thistles, dots of toad lily that look like miniature orchids, and tall fluffy grasses. Around this time of year we also get old man's beard – a fantastic clematis vine with an autumnal touch. It's perfect for weaving through the flowers and the banister rails; we even taped some to the walls.

FLOWER SELECTION

Daucus
Toad lily
Sanguisorba
Grasses
Globe thistles
Astrantia
Old man's beard
Heathers
Scabious seed pods

1

You can either use floral foam blocks taped into trays or floral foam cages. Soak your floral foam and, assuming you are working *in situ*, place the blocks where you'd like to have your arrangements, with either the wide or the narrow face of the block at the front. Here we used a mixture – the wide faces of the blocks at the front on the landing and the narrow faces along the banister rails.

2

Cut your flowers to different heights and start by positioning the tallest flowers at the back of your blocks. Graduate the heights from back to front so that you can see all the different flowers and nothing gets too lost. If guests will be going up and down the staircase, you need to make sure that each arrangement looks just as good from the back as it does from the front, and that all the floral foam is covered. Each flower needs space to look its best, so don't overcrowd the arrangements and keep stepping back to get an overall view of your work.

3

Cut some shorter lengths of flowers and foliage, and position these at the base of each individual arrangement, angling them slightly to cover the foam. Something with a large head or a broad leaf works best here.

4

When you're happy with the position of each arrangement on the staircase, you can start to wind vines, stems of rosehips or foliage around the banister rails to link the pieces together and add to the feeling that the whole arrangement has grown organically around the staircase.

CIDER ARCH

Flowered arches are a fantastic way to display flowers indoors as well as out. Decorated with cut flowers and foliage, this arch makes a beautiful backdrop for a special ceremony or, with people wandering through it, can simply be used to connect two spaces.

Arches are striking and relatively simple to make. They require a lot of flowers and/or foliage so the cost can really mount up, which means you must think carefully about how to get the most impact from your ingredients.

I like my arches to be as full of texture and as natural as possible. In spring, an arch laden with blossom such as spiraea or crab apple looks almost dreamlike. Equally, arches of different-coloured foliages are incredibly dramatic and are a lot more affordable then using lots of roses.

You can also have a lot of fun with the shape; a full, shaggy arch bursting with flowers, berries and vines is quite something but so, too, is an arch with light, delicate elements woven through the structure.

Here I've done a bit of a mix, leaving some of the structure exposed and concentrating certain elements on specific areas. It's all about experimenting and seeing what works for you, the situation, and the flowers and foliage you have at your disposal. I used apple branches scrumped from my dad's garden, and some cultivated crab apples and tall branches with small apples from the flower market.

FLOWER SELECTION

Apple branches

Cultivated crab apples

Golden beech

Hops

Spindleberry

1

If you don't already have an arch in place, you'll need to assemble one and make sure it's securely fastened to the floor or wall so that it doesn't fall over. If your flowers and foliage are very hardy, you might get away without needing soaked moss or floral foam to keep them looking good, but moss and foam can be really useful for attaching your material securely and at interesting angles. Here I've used floral foam cages that I've attached to the arch using cable ties.

2

I added the larger apple varieties first so I could place the juicy ones just where I wanted them. When apples fell off the branches (and they always do!) I simply wired them back in. Once you start adding flowers and foliage, take care not to make the arch front-heavy. Ensure that it's evenly weighted and held in place very securely. As branches are often gnarly and wild, they tend to dictate the shape the installation takes. Some of the branches here were too big to use with the floral foam, so I wired them straight onto the arch; since they are fairly dried up, there's no danger of them drooping.

3

I varied the sizes of the pieces of golden beech I used, so some areas of the arch had thick clumps of golden foliage, and others just a thin thread of leaves. I also made sure that the spindleberry and the little cultivated crab apples didn't get lost in all the foliage.

4

I wove the hops through the arch, blending them in with the golden beech and apples. Be sure to always step back and make sure the shape is working for you and check for any areas of visible floral foam that may need to be covered.

FLOWER BEAM

This is nothing if not decadent. But once you have the structure in place, it's also very simple.

A flower beam is a great way to make use of any beams in a room and, in this instance, it's perfect for connecting the two adjoining spaces and making the overall effect feel more intimate.

A design like this is a lovely way to play with shape and colour on a large, rather linear scale. We would use it for a wedding in a large, lofty space with beams – a barn for instance, or a warehouse space. It also works well for a dinner setting, especially if your guests are eating from sharing platters; instead of crowding the table even more with flowers, you can have them hanging above. You could even hang the arrangement lower to sit above the table, but in this interconnecting space, people needed to be able to walk underneath, so I kept the whole arrangement high.

Autumn brings with it some of the best big-bloom chrysanthemums. Chrysanthemums have a bit of a reputation as tacky garage forecourt flowers, but some beautiful varieties are being bred, especially in England and Japan. These muted, almost blood-orange ones are my favourite recent market finds, but there are fantastic buttery gold and rusty terracotta heirloom chrysanthemums, too.

Around this time of year we also get lots of rosehips in all shapes and sizes. They are bright little jewels that sing of the season and add plenty of texture. Here I've used their rambling shape to break out from the straight line at the base of the arrangement and swoop underneath.

The colour palette here is very fitting for an autumn gathering. It also lends itself well to my favourite dahlia colours. With their endless swirls and painted petals, they look like different flavours of sorbet as they melt beautifully into the surrounding flowers, and especially into the neighbouring roses.

FLOWER SELECTION

Chrysanthemums

Dahlias

Rosehips

Roses

Strawflowers

Achilleas

Apple branches

Beech leaves

Guelder rose foliage

Spindleberry

1

With some strong rope and a sturdy plank of wood, you are off to a great start. Hang the plank from your supporting structure (that can be a beam, like the one I've used for this display, or even a good tree branch if you are outside). Make sure your knots are really secure and your plank is horizontal. The finished arrangement will be very heavy, so be sure to check that your rope and wood are up to the job.

2

Soak your blocks of floral foam and put them in trays along the length of the plank. Tape them to the plank with clear pot tape.

3

Start placing your flowers in the floral foam blocks, concentrating on the shape you want to create and stepping back regularly to check that you're happy with the effect. Remember that the negative space in the design is just as crucial as the flowers, so be sure to leave some gaps in the arrangement so that the overall silhouette isn't too uniform.

4

I use this stage to decide where to place my colours. Here we have shifted from a deep red-grapefruit colour to a pale cream, with apricot, peach and pink linking those two colours together.

5

Now I gradually build the arrangement up, using a mix of flowers and foliage, and gauging the character and movement of the piece as I go. Finally, I place the rosehips and smaller berries for added texture.

AUTUMN FEAST TABLE

This is a take on the harvest table, where the boundaries of flowers and food as decoration are blurred and we can highlight the gems of the season. Everything turns such a good colour at this time of year: the plums have dappled skins and the beans are streaked with muted magenta and chalky white. Instead of going for generic orange pumpkins, look at some of the other varieties available. Pairing flowers and food is a lot of fun and makes for a striking table. You don't have to be very strict about the way you do it, but when you echo a colour from the petal to the plate, the whole setting sings.

As an example of how the flower arrangements don't need to be confined to the vase, I've used pale, porcelain-coloured pumpkins to link with the creamy colours in our flowers and with some of the food on the table.

I've even attached a tiny water source – a thimbleful of water or a wired-on offcut of soaked floral foam – to some of the candlesticks so that flowers can be displayed here, too.

I've also wired fruit branches to some of the candlestick holders and have wound hops and clematis vines around the silverware. With scattered petals and the odd rosehead on the table linen, it all starts to feel very abundant.

FLOWER SELECTION

Hydrangeas

Roses

Statice

Rosehips

Old man's beard

Strawflowers

Astrantia

Dahlias

Hops

Geranium leaves

Achillea

Crab apple branches

Blackberries

1

Start by laying out your flowers and food and look at which ingredients tie in nicely together, making a note of what works with what.

2

For attaching flowers to the candlesticks there are a couple of options. Some of the flowers that last well out of water can be simply wired on (you can cleverly conceal the wire in the nooks and crannies of the silverware) or else you can cut a small piece of soaked floral foam (or use moss and water) and wedge into the tops of the candlestick holders (where the candle would usually be).

3

Not all the candlesticks need to be the same size, so cut some down to give you taller and shorter elements. The central arrangement here, with its larger, more flower-abundant presence, creates some focus, but do what works for you and your table.

4

I've also scattered loose flower heads and other offcuts around the table, as well as adding a small vase arrangement using chicken wire (see page 49 for using chicken wire this way) to blur the boundary of what belongs in a vase and what belongs on a plate. This all helps to make the table feel whole and bountiful.

WINTER

WINTER

Winter doesn't need to be all doom and gloom. There is something quietly magical about the stark outdoors. With lots of aromatic foliages, jewel-like berries and beautiful flowers, winter has its own beauty. Even the bare branches outside have fantastic architectural shapes.

Instead of trying to perk up spaces with loud, bright colours, I prefer to work with the dramatic weather and moody cold light, creating arrangements that capture our wintry surroundings and bring their beauty inside.

Now there is the opportunity to use lots of snowy white blooms like anemones, roses and ranunculus. Paired with the chalky blue of juniper, eucalyptus and spruce, these immediately give a sense of cool wintriness.

It's also a real treat to work with sumptuous, moody tones that capture winter's cosy warmth. There are incredible ranunculus in deep aubergine and almost black cherry, with endless ruffles of petals fading into translucent silver at the edges, not to mention the velvety, dark plum anemones that seem to change colour with every passing day. I sometimes melt these dark tones into juicy accents by softening them with cold blush pinks.

In fact, almost no colour is off limits at this time of year: flowers in shades of yellow and cream can be cool and wintry, too, providing you pair them with the right foliage, for example, pale grey mimosa or eucalyptus.

Then there are the dried flowers left over from the summer seed pods and grasses, vines of old man's beard, catkins and my new favourite, hydrangeas, which, when dried, may consist of nothing more than a few petals resting like butterflies on their spindly stems.

The best part of winter is the unspoken acknowledgement that it's time for the outside to come in. It's the only time of year when nearly everyone has some greenery indoors, from a sprig of holly perched on each and every picture frame to doors hung with wreaths that open onto staircases draped in foliage, fruits and berries, or table centrepieces of winter flowers alongside fireplaces dripping in candles, pine cones and sweet-smelling greenery. As I say, it's not all doom and gloom.

TRADITIONAL WREATH

Wreaths can be made in any season but it's at this festive time of year that they really come into their own. Nearly every front door you pass will have a little circlet of foliage proudly presented. I love the variety and the styles that people display on their doors, and what it says about their tastes and their character. Some people opt for simple greenery and an effortless look, while others will throw every type of ribbon, berry and bauble at their wreath for maximum festive impact. There is no right or wrong when making a wreath, but as a general rule, you want your ingredients to hold out until the end of the festive season, which means choosing hardy foliage that will crisp and dry elegantly with age, rather than sag and wilt.

Here I've made a small wreath, using lots of ingredients that vary in size, shape, colour and texture to showcase some of the best bits of the season. The pine and ferns make a great base, offering plenty of coverage, while still being interesting. Their tips sprawl out to the side, giving the wreath great shape and character. I love the streaks of silver that come from the underside of the grevillea, and the soft blue eucalyptus is a good contrast with all the greens.

I've kept the wreath quite natural with pine cones and berries from the juniper foliage, but if you want some glitz, there are some really fun painted and dyed foliages and dried goods that you can add. I also love using twigs and branches; these give you the opportunity to experiment with shape and create incredibly sculptural wreaths.

FLOWER SELECTION

Umbrella ferns

Ming ferns

Pine foliage and cones

Eucalyptus

Grevillea

Juniper

Birch catkins

Myrtle

Magnolia

1

I've started this wreath with a wire wreath frame and have attached my spool wire to the frame. Holding the spool in one hand, bunch up the moss and wind the wire around the frame to secure the moss in place.

2

Put the wreath to one side and make the foliage into little bundles with all their stems aligned at the bottom. If you want a big bushy wreath, use large swathes of foliage and go all out; for a more detailed, smaller wreath, keep your bundles on the small side. Arrange the larger, bulkier materials at the back of each bundle and the finer, more textured material on top so that you'll be able to see everything once it's in place on the wreath. Secure your bundles with wire or string around the stems.

3

When you attach your bundles to the wreath, be sure to cover as much of the moss as possible. I burrow the stems of each bundle into the moss as close as I can to the inner edge of the wreath. Play with the angles to see what you like the look of, then secure each bundle with spool wire, being sure to work only in one direction and overlapping each bundle on top of the previous one.

4

Continue adding your bundles of foliage all the way around until the wreath is covered with bundles, then snip off the wire leaving a good length. Tie this to the back of the frame and use it to create a small loop to hang your wreath up with.

SCULPTURAL WREATH

There really aren't any rules when it comes to wreaths; what you can and can't use and how big or how small you make your wreath is entirely up to you. This wreath is much more three-dimensional than the Traditional wreath (see page 152).

Its base is made from grapevines instead of moss and I've then added sculptural branches, clusters of seed pods and pine cones, and other interesting foraged bits and pieces.

STAIRCASE GARLAND

There's nothing quite like coming in from the cold and opening the front door onto a staircase dressed in greenery and bathed in warm light. It's a great way to make an entrance for a party or simply to celebrate the festive season.

Depending on the look you want to go for, you can keep the garland tight and trim to make just a small gesture, or have it big and untamed, with swathes of foliage sweeping down the staircase.

To add texture, scent and intrigue to your staircase garland, you can use all sorts of wonderful dried fruits, spices, branches and seed pods. It's a great time of year to forage for interesting forgotten bits in the gardens and hedgerows, but you can also dry your own fruit slices or find them readily available in shops, markets and online.

The great thing about using lots of foliage is the variety you get to work with. There are so many different shades of green and blue and brown and red, so many shapes and textures and rich scents. The endless choice available is part of the beauty.

You could pick out a bit of everything, with the different shades of green creating a richly textured garland of opulent, deep tones, and with highlights of fresh lime-green to break these up. Or, as an alternative, there is something incredibly striking about using a single material – a staircase draped only in glossy sugar pine looks effortless and beautiful.

For practicality, use foliages that will last well out of water or that dry out without wilting, and stay clear of fresh flowers unless you want to adorn your garland with them for a special occasion. If that's the case, they can be placed in floristry water vials and tucked into the foliage or wired into the garland shortly before a party.

Generally speaking, it's a good idea to use a foliage that is big and bushy – that way you get plenty of coverage – but apart from that, just use any interesting bits of foliage that take your fancy.

FLOWER SELECTION

Pine foliage and cones
Cypress
Magnolia
Ferns
Grevillea
Birch catkins
Dried lotus pods
Dried orange slices

Gather up your chosen foliage into mixed bunches. If you want a large, unruly garland, keep the pieces long; for a neater, more refined one, cut them short. If you're using a mix of different greenery, put the heavier, broader pieces at the back and the more detailed, delicate elements at the front, otherwise you won't be able to see them. Secure each bunch with string, elastic bands, wire or tape. Cut a length of rope to fit your banister rail and attach the bunches of foliage to the rope with string, starting at what will be one end of your garland.

2

When you attach one bunch, you want to cover the string you've used to attach the previous bunch – known as the bind point. Keep working your way along the rope like this. If you're aiming for a more contained and delicate garland, then you don't need to make the greenery into bunches; instead, just attach the pieces of foliage individually but still take care to cover the bind points of the previous pieces.

3

When you've covered the length of rope, it's time to attach the garland to the staircase. You're options here really depend on the type of staircase you have. I've attached this garland to the balusters with cable ties but if you don't have balusters (you might have glass or wooden panels instead) you could attach the garland to the banister rail itself.

4

Finish by adding any little details you fancy. Here I wired in some pine cones, lotus pods and dried orange slices, but you can use beautiful ribbons, dried or fresh flowers for a special occasion, or anything else you like.

MANTELPIECE GARLAND

The great thing about garlands is their versatility. Whether you have them snaking down the length of a dinner table, cascading over a doorway or draped across a mantelpiece like this one, they make a fantastic base to which it's easy to add fresh flowers for a special occasion.

FLOWER SELECTION

Magnolia blossom
Cherry blossom
Blush roses
Astrantia
Ranunculus
Anemones
Waxflowers
Viburnum berries
Mimosa foliage

ARRANGEMENT

Using the same method as for the Staircase garland (see page 167), I made a simple garland of smoky blue and purple mimosa foliage, with bright pink dots of fragrant waxflowers and tiny, jewel-like viburnum berries to add texture. We were fortunate enough to have an incredibly mild winter, so we were able to get the first magnolia and cherry blossom very early. Their beautiful mix of soft pink, magenta and brown was the inspiration for this arrangement.

You can either use little floristry water vials to 'post' stems of flowers and berries through the foliage or, for a more dramatic arrangement like this one, floral foam or small vases strategically placed along the mantelpiece. I used varying sized blocks of floral foam. With my basic garland of mimosa foliage in place on the mantelpiece, I started by adding some large branches of magnolia in floral foam blocks to add depth and shape. I then began filling out the garland with more mimosa foliage and, finally, I added my flowers. The rich colours from the mimosa and waxflower base provide the opportunity for a really sumptuous palette of deep magenta pinks, black cherry and soft berry ice-cream tones. The finished arrangement has a very decadent, wintry feel to it.

GIFT TOPPERS

Let's be honest, wrapping gifts to put under the Christmas tree can be a competitive family sport. From who has found the prettiest paper to who has made their own, it's game time. If you want something a little extra special rather than the usual paper and string parcels, then these little gift toppers are incredibly festive and very easy to make.

FLOWER SELECTION

Pine cones

Fresh peppercorns

Cherry blossom

Magnolia buds

Myrtle

Waxflowers

1

You can attach the gift toppers to your packages with either glue or string. To attach them with string, first tie a length of string around a small piece of dry floral foam.

2

Start by adding the bulkier bits of foliage around the edges of your dry foam, keeping the base of the foam bare so it will sit flat on your gift.

3

Add your finer details like berries and baby pine cones towards the top so they can be easily seen. Check for visible floral foam and if you find any, cover it with some foliage or other material.

4

Secure the topper to your gift with glue or string. If you've gone big, you might need a blob of glue as well as the string.

WINTER TABLE

Whether you're throwing a dinner party, having friends over for coffee or just want your dining table to look extra special, nothing beats having some floral focus. There's something a little unceremonious about unwrapping a pack of roses from the supermarket and plonking them in a vase. So, to bring a touch of seasonal nature to your table, go outside and snip some foliage or flowers to add to your purchase.

My favourite way to arrange flowers is to follow the natural shape of the stems and foliage. This accentuates their form and creates an arrangement that feels as if it's grown out of the vase.

FLOWER SELECTION

Eucharis

Blackthorn blossom

Juniper

Myrtle

Ferns

Anemones

Roses

Flowering chives

Cherry blossom

Vibernum

Muscari

Ranunculus

Spray roses

ARRANGEMENT

With this centrepiece I have gone with a wintry white palette and used some of the best snippets of the season. Ranunculus may be my all-time favourite flower. Perhaps. I love their never-ending petals that unfurl and become more translucent and papery by the day. I've used a mix of shapes and textures in this arrangement; the curving stems of chives create a lovely profile and the roses in their various shapes and sizes draw the eye in and around the whole arrangement. I've paired some of the obvious Christmas foliages like pine with interesting finds like juniper and myrtle branches, complete with their berries. If you are enjoying a mild winter, you might be lucky enough to find some blackthorn blossom while you're out and about. I did, so I have studded the arrangement with these delicate little flowers for added texture.

1

To secure the stems, either cut a piece of soaked floral foam to size or ball up some chicken wire (see page 49 for using chicken wire this way). Place in a water-filled vase but don't use a glass vase, or the floral foam or chicken wire will be visible.

2

Think about your vase and the shape you want your arrangement. I built up the shape around the sweeping branches of blackthorn and the curling stems of chives. Then I started adding my mix of foliages and flowers, and thought about where I wanted the focal points to be.

3

Next I started to fill the arrangement out with myrtle and juniper, and began to place the larger-headed flowers, like the ranunculus and roses.

4

With a clearer picture of my arrangement's shape, I know where to place my focal flowers – the eucharis – to create balance and draw the eye. Your focal flowers don't necessarily need to be the biggest but try not to dot them too evenly around the arrangement. Here, the star shape of the eucharis stands out among the soft, blousy petals of the roses and ranunculus. I love how one of the eucharis flowers curls back over the rim of the vase, breaking up the line between vase and arrangement.

GLOSSARY

Chicken wire

An invaluable element for flower arranging, this comes in a variety of weights and hole sizes. Use it for supporting stems in a vase and for wrapping around floral foam shapes. You will need chicken wire when working on the following projects in this book, but you will find it useful in any vase-based arrangements (as long as the vase is opaque), or as added support for all your floral foam-based projects.

Conditioning

Your flowers and foliage will last longer if you condition them before arranging them. Trim the stems with a sharp knife, floristry scissors or secateurs by at least 2.5cm (1in), cutting them at an angle to expose the maximum surface area for the uptake of water. Give them a deep drink of lukewarm water. If you have to re-trim the stems as you arrange them, again cut them at an angle and always with a sharp knife. Remove any foliage that will be under water, as this will rot and produce bacteria that will shorten the life of your arrangement. Also remove foliage from any part of the stem that will be embedded in floral foam. Conditioning flowers and foliage benefits all the projects in this book as your material will last longer, but it's essential for the Table meadow (see page 52), and is the main technique you need for the following projects:

Floral foam

Essential for arranging your flowers, this comes in a green version for holding fresh flowers and a brown version for dried flowers. You can buy it in pieces that you cut to shape and size with a sharp knife, as well as in pre-cut shapes or ready fitted into trays and cage-like frames. You must soak the green version before you use it. To do this, float it in a deep bowl or bucket of water until it sinks to the bottom and air bubbles stop escaping. Do not push the foam down. Leave it to stand in a sink until the excess water has drained out, then it's ready to use. You cannot use it twice; if you try to re-soak the foam and use it for another arrangement, it will fall to pieces. Floral foam is key for building floral displays that don't involve using a vase. You will need it for the following projects:

Table meadow 52
Flower chandelier 66
Chair decoration 84
Living staircase 116
Cider arch 124

Flower beam 132
Autumn feast table 138
Mantelpiece garland 168
Gift toppers 172
Winter table 180

Hand tying

This technique is used when building stand-alone bouquets and vase arrangements. My preferred method is to start by holding one stem of foliage and to place a single focal flower on top, crossing the stems over. Gradually add stem after stem of foliage and flowers, crossing each stem over the last and always working in the same direction to create an even spiral of stems and flowers. Hold your stems firmly at the bind point (the point where the stems cross over each other – giving your arrangement strength) as you go. When I've added all the plant material, I like to tease out a few stems so the arrangement doesn't look too neat. Finish by trimming the ends of the stems to the same length and tie at the bind point, using your preferred method. This technique gets easier with practice. Use it to make the following projects:

Flowers to give as a gift 32 | Bridal bouquet 108

Taping

Use waterproof adhesive tape (sometimes called pot tape) for securing wet floral foam to trays and vases, for taping cut ends of flowers and foliage so they last longer, and for holding bunches of flowers and foliage together. The tape comes in a variety of widths. You will need floral tape for the following projects:

Flower crown 24	Festival flower crown 90
Buttonholes 76	Flower beam 132

Wiring

This involves either supporting a stem with floral wire, creating a stem for a flower head or flower pip, or attaching flowers, foliage or moss to an arrangement or frame (a wreath frame, for example). You can use spool wire (wire on a reel) or stub wires (pre-cut lengths of wire) in a variety of thicknesses. Choose your wire according to what you want to use it for. Wiring is key for many projects. In this book, you will need it to construct the following projects:

Flower crown 24	Traditional wreath 152
Buttonholes 76	Sculptural wreath 158
Festival flower crown 90	Staircase garland 162
Cider arch 124	Mantelpiece garland 168
Autumn feast table 138	

PLANT DIRECTORY

Achillea/*Achillea* spp 68, 69, 99, 111, 135, 143

Allium/*Allium* spp 26, 27, 77, 79

Anemone/*Anemone* spp 57, 149, 170, 182

Apple/*Malus* spp 40, 57, 69, 86, 87, 99, 126, 127, 129, 135

Apple, Crab/*Malus sylvestris* 126, 127, 129, 143

Aquilegia/*Aquilegia* spp 57

Astrantia/*Astrantia* spp 119, 143, 170

Beech/*Fagus* spp 127, 129, 135

Birch/*Betula* spp 155, 165

Blackthorn/*Prunus spinosa* 21, 182, 183, 185

Cherry/*Prunus* spp 21, 170, 171, 175, 182

Chive/*Allium schoenoprasum* 35, 182, 183, 185

Chrysanthemum/*Chrysanthemum* spp 26, 105, 134, 135

Clematis/*Clematis* spp 26, 27, 79, 101, 118, 141

Cosmos/*Cosmos* spp 63, 97, 99

Cypress/*Cupressus* spp 165

Daffodil/*Narcissus* spp 21, 35, 57

Dahlia/*Dahlia* spp 63, 68, 86, 87, 99, 105, 111, 134, 135, 143

Daucus/*Daucus carota* 118, 119

Dicentra/*Dicentra* spp 17, 40, 41

Dill/*Anethum graveolens* 99

Echinacea/*Echinacea* spp 87, 99

Eucalyptus/*Eucalyptus* spp 26, 27, 34, 35, 79, 149, 154, 155

Eucharis/*Eucharis* spp 182, 185

Fern, Ming/*Asparagus macowanii* 155

Fern, Umbrella/*Sticherus cunninghamii* 155

Foxglove/*Digitalis* spp 35, 40, 46, 47

Fritillary/*Fritillaria* spp 17, 26, 27, 35, 40, 41, 57, 79

Guelder rose/*Viburnum opulus* 35

Geranium/*Pelargonium* spp 46, 47, 86, 87, 99, 143

Grevillea/*Grevillea* spp 154, 155, 165

Heather/*Calluna, Erica* spp 119

Hellebore/*Helleborus* spp 26, 40, 57

Honeysuckle/*Lonicera* spp 55

Hops/*Humulus lupulus* 105, 127, 129, 141, 143

Hornbeam/*Carpinus* spp 69, 87, 99

Hydrangea/*Hydrangea* spp 68, 105, 111, 143, 149

Jasmine/*Jasminum* spp 46, 47, 87, 101

Juniper/*Juniperus* spp 149, 154, 155, 182, 183, 185

Larkspur/*Delphinium* spp 35, 77

Lily, toad/*Tricyrtis hirta* 118, 119

Lisianthus/*Eustoma* spp 26, 111

Love-in-a-mist/*Nigella* spp 35, 99

Magnolia/*Magnolia* spp 155, 165, 170, 171, 175

Marigold/*Tagetes* spp 63, 87, 99

Mimosa/*Mimosa* spp 111, 149, 170, 171

Mock orange/*Philadelphus* spp 35, 55, 57

Muscari/*Muscari* spp 182

Myrtle/*Myrtus* spp 26, 155, 175, 182, 183, 185

Old man's beard/*Clematis vitalba* 118, 119, 143, 149

Passion flower/*Passiflora* spp 101

Peony/*Paeonia* spp 17, 21, 26, 35, 46, 47, 55, 57, 63, 68, 69

Pine/*Pinus* spp 149, 154, 155, 159, 164, 167, 175, 177, 183

Poppy/*Papaver* spp 57

Prunus/*Prunus* spp 69

Ranunculus/*Ranunculus* spp 35, 40, 41, 57, 149, 170, 182, 183, 185

Rose/*Rosa* spp 8, 17, 26, 27, 34, 39, 40, 46, 47, 55, 57, 63, 68, 69, 77, 79, 86, 87, 105, 110, 111, 118, 121, 126, 134, 135, 137, 141, 143, 149, 170, 181, 182, 183, 185

Rosemary/*Rosmarinus officinalis* 26, 85

Sanguisorba/*Sanguisorba* spp 26, 118, 119

Scabious/*Scabiosa* spp 17, 63, 97, 99, 118, 119

Spiraea/*Spiraea* spp 21, 26, 27, 40, 55, 57, 79, 126

Statice/*Limonium* spp 143

Spindleberry/*Euonymus europaeus* 127, 129, 135

Spruce/*Picea* spp 149

Strawflower/*Xerochrysum bracteatum* 26, 109, 111, 135, 143

Sweet pea/*Lathyrus odoratus* 35, 40, 46, 47, 69, 87, 99, 101

Tanacetum daisies/*Tanacetum* spp 69, 99

Tulip/*Tulipa* spp 35, 40, 57

Verbena/*Verbena* spp 63

Viburnum/*Viburnum* spp 26, 170

Waxflower/*Chamelaucium* spp 26, 78, 85, 170, 171, 175

THANK YOU

To the guys and girls at Petalon

Thank you for making it such a joyous place to work over the past couple of years and for helping me build something that I am so proud of.

Becki Willmore for running such a tight ship, keeping me sane and giving me the time and space to write this book.

Aisling Maye for your unwavering hard work and dedication to the floral cause. Your vision and work ethic are beautiful things.

Orlagh Wright for making me laugh until I cry, keeping me calm when the work gets intense and always making me smile with your stunning designs.

Alex Whitmore for always going above and beyond in whatever you do. It's been the greatest pleasure discovering flowers with you. Thank you for inspiring me to think carefully about colours and for giving me the chance to fall in love with flowers with you. I could not ask for a better 4am friend.

Billie Rimmer for your patience and dedication to Petalon as we grew, from our first roots to our finest moments. Thank you.

Sam Fox for your willingness to help whenever we are in need. The studio at 7am is a better place to be with you around.

To the book team

India Hobson, my photographer, thank you for capturing my flowers so beautifully. It's a pleasure to watch you work in a medium you love so much.

Laura Russell, Alexander Breeze, Hilary Mandleberg, Sophie Yamamoto, Katie Hewett, and everyone at Pavilion who has worked on the book, thank you for your input. And Krissy Mallett my wonderful editor, thank you for asking me to make this book with you. Your never-ending patience and constant support have been incredible and I am so lucky to have you.

To my suppliers

Everyone at New Covent Garden Market, Sian at Lancaster & Cornish for always providing me with beautiful ribbons, and Holly at The Floury for all the delicious cakes in this book.

To my family

Ingrid Hill, my mum, for your love of art and design and for fuelling my creativity throughout my life, from taking me to exhibitions when I was little and doing art projects on the kitchen table with me, to sending me inspiring magazine articles once I'd left home. Thank you for being so fiercely proud of me. You gave me the confidence to go my own way. I am a very lucky daughter.

Stephen Hill, my dad, for giving me a corner of your vegetable patch and showing me how to grow flowers, and for taking me to places of such incredible natural beauty around the world. Thank you for feeding my passion for nature.

Susie Mee, my Bomma. Your endless hard work and independence have always been an inspiration to me. Thank you for supporting me no matter which way I have gone and for being on the other end of the phone to share your pearls of wisdom when I needed them most

Ian and Nicky Kennedy. There has never been a luckier person than me to get in-laws like you. Whatever path James and I have taken, you have always helped us on our way. Thank you for your constant love and support, and for welcoming me into your caring, wonderful family.

James Kennedy, thank you for everything. Your enthusiasm for life is contagious and I wouldn't ever have considered the possibility of Petalon without your encouragement. Thanks to you I have flowers – and so much more than I ever dreamed possible. You make life extraordinary and I love living it with you.

First published in the United Kingdom in 2017 by
Pavilion
43 Great Ormond Street
London
WC1N 3HZ

ISBN 978-1-911216-30-8

A CIP catalogue record for this book is available from the British Library.

10 9 8 7 6 5 4 3 2 1

Reproduction by Mission Productions Ltd, Hong Kong
Printed and bound by 1010 Printing International Ltd, China

This book can be ordered direct from the publisher at
www.pavilionbooks.com